DON'T
BOX
ME
IN

2ND EDITION

Marcellus C. Taylor, D.Ed.

For More Copies & Author Engagements , Contact

Blossburg & Cedar LLC

Email : grow@blossburgandcedar.com

Dedication

The second edition of this book is dedicated to the dreamers and doers who have faith to believe that tomorrow will be filled with a greater level of purpose and progress.

Acknowledgements

I want to acknowledge my wife Denise T. Taylor your love is a great motivator and a sustaining force. To MLK, daddy loves you and hopes this book will inspire you to change the world!

CONTENTS

INTRODUCTION

When my wife suggested that I should of write a second edition of this book, I instantly began to idea-cast of all the ways I might share new insight almost seven years after publishing the 1st edition. Over the course of several months I have read, re-read and edited every sentence in this book. You will see that I still believe that we all have a voice and that our voice is vital to the success of others. This book should be used as a road map to discover or rediscover who you are and what you were born to do.

There are several new features in the book that I believe will help guide you to a better version of you. In each chapter you will find IN-PROMPT-YOU Moments and Make-It- Happen Maps. IN-PROMPT-YOU Moments are deep probing questions that will ask you to explore the future and bring that wisdom into the present. Make-It-Happen Maps are step-by-step guides that you will create to bring the lessons learned in this book to life.

I Heard an Old Man Say ...

This book was conceived out of ease dropping! I was utilizing public transportation in Philadelphia (my hometown), and heard the greatest advice ever. An older man with a ridiculously long gray beard was babbling to a group of energetic teenagers seemingly coming from school. The teenagers tried their hardest to move away from the old man but were stuck listening to his "wise" words because the bus was beyond crowed. The words that came out of his mouth would forever shape my view on leadership.

He said with wise assurance, "never discredit the power of your voice". I was instantly pierced at my core. I felt that I was on this specific bus, on this specific day at this particular time to hear this particular old man share this profound message .The word "voice" began to ring in my head for the rest of the day. I began to write my definition of the term voice on the back of a receipt that was in my wallet. My definition for the word voice is below,

"Your unique expression of your gifts and talents"

The old man was giving the youth a life lesson that I hope to communicate with you over the next several chapters of this book. The old man instructed the teens to never discredit the power of their voice because they were born to be a solution to someone's problem. You were born to be an answer to someone's problem. Your birth was the answer to a prayer, hope and dream of a person or people in need.

If Mahatma Ghandi would have discredited his voice, India could still be under British rule. If Maya Angelou would have discredited the power of her voice we would not have known why the caged bird sings. If Martin Luther King would have discredited the power of his voice we could still be living in the nightmare of Jim and Jane Crow. Like the above mentioned iconic figures it is critical for you to ALWAYS keep at the forefront of your mind that your voice is a tool to get others to see the totality of their potential.

If you were to take a survey of all of the leaders and mentors that have inspired you, I would make a bet that they shared a common quality found in all creative leaders, the ability to reimagine the world around them. They all refused to be BOXED IN! They do not fit the conventional mode or use common methods to be a leader. Each day they make a firm commitment remain on the outside of the "box". The "box" is the home of comfortable living, fear and averageness. Today you have to decide to step out of the "box" or you may bare its fruit which is mediocrity, complacency and failure.

This book will give you practical steps for being a creative leader in any environment that you enter. First we will explore the three characteristics of having an effective voice. Next we will investigate the common pitfalls of creative leaders. Lastly, we will look at three methods that will aid you in your journey to become an unboxed leader. Being an achiever is about replicating your success and constantly perfecting your skills. Don't Box Me In, is your personal guide to becoming the purpose-led person you want to be. Before we move forward, I need you to repeat after me,

"TODAY I WILL STEP OUT OF THE BOX AND CREATE MY FUTURE."

Your Voice

"Your voice has a purpose, gives you power and provides you a platform."

Chapter 1

Purpose

When a caterpillar is born it is instantly on a path to becoming a high flying butterfly. The butterfly's future will not be that of a pestering mosquito, a flustering moth or an energize gnat. Like the aforementioned insects the butterfly has the faculties to fly, but despite this commonality of flying a butterfly has a different life cycle. This difference is called purpose.

PURPOSE: the object towards which one strives; or for which something exist.

What is your purpose? What causes you to work hard daily without recognition? To answer these two critical questions you have to first believe that you are a unique individual with special gifts and talents. Yes, you got it, **YOU HAVE A VOICE!** Inside of you are million dollar ideas brewing and ready to be released. You are the missing link to someone's puzzle. Your birth was for a radiant purpose.

I was in search of good music lyrics that would help me better illustrate what it looks like to live on purpose and I found a stanza from an amazing artist from the past that will help shed light on understanding purpose today. The lyrics below are captivating;

9

"If I can help somebody, as I pass along,

If I can cheer somebody, with a word or a song,

If I can show somebody, how they're traveling wrong,

Then my living shall not be in vain" – Mahalia Jackson

The late great Mahalia Jackson reminds us that our purpose is often connected to empowering others which in turn will give us more strength to live a life of greatness marked by consistent wins. We all have the capacity to "help somebody". We began to discover our purpose when we resolve to uplift and empower broken and depleted situation. The requirements of being a person who lives on purpose are simple, you only have to be alive. If you are alive you have the tools within you to live on **PURPOSE**.

10

You may now be wondering, when will we get to the part of the book where we learn how to practically make this happen? I am glad you have arrived at this question, but before we discuss practical steps I want to share an amazing story with you about a leader who had the audacity to believe that living on purpose was better than going with the motions of a life filled with averageness.

I now direct your attention to the capital city of Harrisburg, Pennsylvania. The year is 2015 and a women with the leadership potential to head any fortune five hundred company decides that "today is the last day I will fulfil the norms and career paths placed on me" based on "standard" that were set without me in mind. This embolden leader has a vision that has been developing in her since her youth. She imagined a learning environment that gave children the tools needed to learn and growth despite the contextual obstacles that they may face.

With the support of close friends and the assistance of a real estate agent determined to find the perfect location for this new child learning oasis, this leader found a building and began to generate marketing material for parents to enroll their children . She had the faith and fortitude of a great army. This leader found the sweet spot of purpose that energizes and creates a never ending flood of hope. Her name is Denise Taylor and I have the privilege of being her husband and best friend.

Step 1: Find Your Purpose

Finding your purpose is not the easiest of human endeavors. Please do not slam this book down if you feel that you are at the age where you should know your purpose, or you are too young to know your purpose. In fact you are reading the right book! Many people will suggest taking millions of test to discover what you were born to do. I believe these test often do not fully get to the depth of your purpose.

I believe that if you want to find your purpose it will require you to do some work. Noticed the phrase is not "look for your purpose", it is "find your purpose". You must actively search and search again until you find that thing that is worth losing sleep and friends over. All creative leaders must find a purpose before they can reach their peak of greatness.

Step 2: Work Your Purpose

Once you find your purpose, you must begin to work your purpose. To work your purpose is to actively use it in any arena you find yourself in. Let's look at a basic example of working your purpose. Imagine that your purpose is to be a painter. I must admit that painting is not my purpose but I do enjoy its creative lure.

The painter must continually search for avenues to carry out their life vocation. They may decide to teach painting at a local community center or they can raise funds to have their own art exhibit. They could also enroll in an art school to thoroughly perfect their craft. The point is that they are working their purpose. You must not stop working your purpose your purpose is calling you 24/7.

Remember that all creative leaders have a purpose. They do not stop at the limitations of their skills and talents! They have a greater pull towards greatness and success. Without purpose your accomplishments are merely a collection of single records. You will be known for a few hits songs but never a stellar album. I challenge you today to begin to live your life on purpose.

Make-It-Happen Map 1

In the next 30 days , I will do the following to maximize my purpose 1. 2.	What resources are needed to accomplish these goals?
In the next 60 days , I will do the following to maximize my purpose 1. 2.	What resources are needed to accomplish these goals?
In the next 90 days , I will do the following to maximize my purpose 1. 2.	What resources are needed to accomplish these goals?

Chapter 2

Power

Perhaps one of the greatest words in the entire

English language is the word power. The Greeks use

the word dunamis to describe the process of

performing in an extravagant way. They further define

dunamis as a state of acting in a capacity embolden

by strength, power and ability. Dunamis is the term

that the English word dynamite derives from. When I hear the word dynamite, I instantly think of heavy explosives of an epic magnitude. I remember as a teenager watching a high-rise housing complex being torn down. The demolition company decided to use explosives to accomplish this massive project because they realized that larger structures require large amounts of power to accomplish the demolition. This analogy relates to all of us in that we all have large structures in our lives, communities and society at large that will require us to address them with strong power.

POWER: is the ability to do or the capability of doing or accomplishing something.

Imagine your voice as dynamite. When you use your unique expression of your gifts and talents you are creating an explosion. This explosion eradicates mediocrity and blows away behemoth size averageness. The reason why dynamite is so explosive is not simply because of its inner parts but also because it has a fuse. If there is not an avenue for the volatile material to be charged, there will be no explosion. You must be wondering what a fuse and volatile material has to do with power?

To answer your question about the connectivity between a fuse, volatile material and power, the answer is a resounding EVERYTHING! To create an explosion you need a cord for the fire to travel to expose material to generate power. For power to work in your life, you must have a channel for the spark to hit the material. Or better stated, power can only happen when you combine passion (the spark) with talent (the cord) and opportunity (the material).

The Spark

Every awesome idea begins with a spark, an ignition of a thought. The thought could be to solve world poverty or eliminate bullying in your local middle school. No matter the thought, passion is needed to begin to make a large impact into the endeavor. Passion gives you the initial kick start to get the ball moving with your initial thought. Passion led my friend Elaine Johnson to create Latinas in Motion, a non-profit that was organized to inspire, encourage, and empower women to run. Her passion has turned into a national movement that continues to deposit determination, purpose and accountability into the lives of each woman the organization serves.

The Cord

So you guessed it right, a spark without a cord is pointless. Your cord is the perfectly bounded talents and qualities that allow your passion to reach your opportunities which create a large boom! I want you to do a quick inventory of your talents I know that

you must be grinning because you have so many.
Write your top three talents below:

1.

2.

3.

Now, I want you to think for a moment how you can
combine passion with the talents you listed to change
the world. Mother Teresa of Calcutta had a passion to
eliminate poverty and suffering in desolate places in
India. Her talents of administration and service, led
her to create the Missionaries of Charity. The
Missionaries of Charity is an organization dedicated to
the noble mission of advancing the plight of people in
poverty. The organization is still in existence years

after its inception because of the power that was used to birth the original concept of the organization.

The Material

Perhaps the most complicated and delicate aspect of the threefold combination is the material that makes up the explosive package. Opportunities are essential for you to be a powerful creative leader without them you will be sitting on a field of potential energy. Potential energy is energy that is stored up in an object. Potential energy has the ability to do work but falls short when it is time to capitalize on that ability. Opportunities allow you the privilege to use your energy for real transformation. You may say that your current life situation is filled with limited opportunities which may be true, however every opportunity gives you the material to make an explosion. **Always remember that limited opportunities do not mean limited power!**

To get a better understanding of what power can look like, I draw from the words and vison of a man who walked boldly with power,

"I have the audacity to believe that people everywhere can have three meals a day for their bodies, education and culture for their minds and dignity, equality and freedom for their spirits."

- Rev. Martin Luther King Jr.

Chapter 3

Platform

Seven years ago when the 1st edition of this book was published my view of an effective platform was limited to the world of education because that was the only world that I could focus on as a newly minted college graduate (**WE ARE**). Now that I have matured and my experiences have been plentiful, I want to offer a new framework for understanding the role that platforms play in our development as creative leaders.

PLATFORM: a declaration of the principles on which a group of persons stands; a place for public discussion.

Social media's impact on society has increased over the last several years. With only using two hundred and fifty characters millions of people can be impacted in a myriad of ways. More videos are being shared, more content is being read and more people are using social media as a means of expression and connectivity. Despite the clear influence of social media, I believe that your platform is more complex than your digital presence.

Your platform is about your audience both in-person and digitally and how they interact with what you communicate. You can be a leader in the same space as someone else but your platforms may be higher and have a greater level of amplification. An example I recently observed was a social media post about wealth. One of my "friends" shared the post and received a decent amount of likes and comments. Another "friend" shared the same post and their post had over ninety shares and hundreds of comments. I should note that the second "friend" in this example had fewer followers than the first individual.

The point I am making is that your following alone does not enhance or devalue your platform. You may have a podcast that has thirty listeners and you are tempted to call it quits because of the size of the audience. You may be an artist who has inconsistent sales for your masterpieces. In both of the aforementioned cases I offer you three words of liberation, **KEEP ON GOING!** Before you tackle bigger platforms be consistent with the one you currently have. There is a group of people who need the solutions you provide. No matter the platform or place of influence you have to use it to grow people into who they were designed to be.

The Challenges

"Be mindful of the most common challenges to your creative leadership which are procrastination, pessimism and personal gain."

Chapter 4

Procrastination

Every day millions of ordinary people have

extraordinary ideas that will revolutionize the way we

live our lives. They write down their thoughts and they

even go as far as to type an electronic copy of the

idea. They become bold enough to send it to all of

their close friends and family. Let's say the idea was a

new software solution that would allow individuals to connect with other community members for local service projects. The person who envisioned this impactful idea decides to put it off until the summer because they claim they will have more time to concentrate on this idea at that time.

PROCRATINATION: to put off doing something especially out of habitual carelessness or laziness.

Once the summer arrives they realize that other life issues interfere with their perfectly planned intentions. Now they push it off until the following fall once again claiming they will definitely have time on Saturdays in the fall to specifically devote to this now fleeting idea. You guessed it right, they never get around to it in the fall because their job has some new additional responsibilities.

What happened to the energy and enthusiasm that

this person had for this amazing idea? What pushed it back a year from its formation in their mind? What force was behind the stagnation of this once big dream? The answer to all of these relevant questions is the great pitfall of procrastination. Procrastination has a way of killing innovation slowly and secretly before we move forward.

Journey with me as I share with you a tiny poem that a dear mentor gave to me when I arrived as a first-year college student;

"If not you then who, if not here then where, if not now than when."

The above saying is simple but it provides insight into how to overcome procrastination. First, **YOU** have to be willing to work madly until the idea comes to life. Secondly, to eliminate procrastination, you must make the idea a part of your daily existence. Lastly, you have to be willing to push further than your energy allows to see the idea come to fruition.

I encourage you to write the vision of your idea on a large poster board and place it in a noticeable spot in your living area. Every time you get a new discovery, write it on the poster board. You have to make the success of your ideas a daily priority in order for them to blossom. Make it a daily habit like drinking coffee or checking your email. Your day should feel incomplete if you have not developed the idea. When your ideas are stimulated daily your creativity will be endless.

IN-PROMPT-YOU Moment 1

In what ways might you overcome areas of procrastination in your life?

(Write your answer below)

Chapter 5

Pessimism

In most groups, organizations and association there's always an individual known for their chronic case of negative sentiments about everything. If they misplaced something their first assumption is that someone must've stolen it. If you come to them with an issue they say it will never work out. They are the coworker that gives off the impression that life was only meant to maximize pain and problem. In all of these cases, I can assure you that pessimism is at work.

PESSIMISM: an inclination to emphasize adverse aspects conditions and possibilities or to expect the worst possible outcome.

As a creative leader you must not fall into the snare of negative thinking. I believe our thoughts will become our "things" if we consistently focus on them. In real time, if you constantly say I am a failure, you are aligning yourself up to believe that damaging lie and it will lead you to your demise. Your attitude about your leadership will affect the size and scope of the impact you have on the world. Trust me!

Winston Churchill once noted to a group of reporters that, **"attitude is a little thing that makes a big difference."** Do not entertain calls from within or externally that oppose the brighter, better and bolder image of who you are as a creative leader. Stand firm in this affirmation;

"I was born to be a radiant, resilient and ready creative leader."

Today has to be the last day you doubt your abilities. You are still alive because you are a solution to an unsolved problem. Situate yourself around friends and family who frequently celebrate and encourage who you were called to be. I am thankful for Denise, Ariel, Gibran, Todd and Candace who all radiantly remind me of my purpose.

Chapter 6

Personal Gain

One of the saddest realities of living in a microwave generation is the expectation of instant gratification and personal gain. Everyone wants to be the lead role in the play no one wants to be a part of the supporting cast. I believe that you should want the best out of life and in fact it's a normal thing to want to better your current state of living. In this chapter I am highlighting personal gain as it pertains to the act of being selfish and self-seeking.

PERSONAL GAIN: seeking success for oneself through ill intentions.

Every creative leader should have a burning desire to transform the world through their voice. If you are only seeking the cars, riches and celebrity status than you are motivated by personal gain. All memorable creative leaders dedicate their lives to advancing the plight of those who are under their purview. They focus on solving problems for groups that need their dedication and passion in order to live life at the next level of abundance.

Mahatma Gandhi illuminated this point amazingly when he proclaimed, **"the best way to find yourself is to lose yourself in the service of others."** Let's be honest, this concept is easier said than done. For many of us it is easier to simply worry about our personal achievements and career. We are taught in many ways that this is a dog-eat-dog world and we must lookout for ourselves. We are also instructed to believe that we are the only ones we should have allegiance to. This mindset is detrimental to all creative leaders.

What if Maya Angelo never wrote the phenomena masterpiece "Still I Rise"? The poem has allowed millions of men and women suffering from oppression, discrimination and low self-esteem to rise from the shadows of their past. She could have kept the poem in her journal and only use it within the context of her own life but instead she released the poem to the world for all to cling to a piece of hope from its lyrical content.

I submit to you that if you want to be an effective leader you have to be a person who selflessly gives loves and support in a greater way. Living in this manner can be difficult and lonely but it will add meaning to your life. If you live just for personal gain, you are simply erasing your name from the great wall people who knelt down to scoop someone up who were wayward from their purpose.

To wrap up this chapter I want to close with the famous story of an individual who denied personal gain for the well-being of a stranger.

[30] "A man was going down from Jerusalem to Jericho and fell into the hands of robbers. They stripped him, beat him up, and fled, leaving him half dead. [31] A priest happened to be going down that road. When he saw him, he passed by on the other side. [32] In the same way, a Levite, when he arrived at the place and saw him, passed by on the other side. [33] But a Samaritan on his journey came up to him, and when he

saw the man, he had compassion. [34] He went over to him and bandaged his wounds, pouring on olive oil and wine. Then he put him on his own animal, brought him to an inn, and took care of him. [35] The next day[a] he took out two denarii,[b] gave them to the innkeeper, and said, 'Take care of him. When I come back I'll reimburse you for whatever extra you spend.'

[36] "Which of these three do you think proved to be a neighbor to the man who fell into the hands of the robbers?"

Luke 10:30-36 (Christian Standard Bible)

Make

It

Happen

"To make your creative leadership effective, you must practice, polish and perpetuate your shills and talents."

Chapter 7

Practice

Now that you have explored the beauty of finding your

voice, and the seriousness of the challenges that can

limited your creative leadership, it is time to **make it**

happen. The first part that you need to make it

happen is to practice. We live in a society that likes to

show up to the game without doing any practice.

Millions of people believe that raw talent is sufficient

for accomplishing all of their hopes and dreams.

PRACTICE: the actual application or use of an

idea, belief, or method.

Something magical happens when you begin to

develop your gifts and talents through the discipline of

practice. The boxer does not simply wake up and

become the heavyweight champion of the world. They

must first build up a suitable level of energy and

endurance. From that level they must begin to master

the basics of boxing including fighting techniques and

adjusting their reflexes. Next a boxer goes into an

intense period of training often between five to seven

hours a day to develop the character and skills

commonly found within champion fighter.

"Practice does not make perfect only perfect practice makes perfect." - Vince Lombardi

The boxer teaches us a great lesson about the importance of practice. Practice allows the boxer to master the craft and develop a high level of confidence. What amount of time do you give to your craft? The boxer wakes up at the crack of dawn to run ten miles and then head to the gym. Once they get to the gym they hit the punching bag for thirty minutes to work on their hand-eye coordination. All of these intense activities happen before they enter the boxing ring.

Notice there was a series of hours dedicated to perfecting their boxing craft before they ever entered the ring. We marvel at the tremendous talent and superb skills without seeing the preparation leading up to the fight. **We often see people when they are in the ring stage of their success and not the training stage.**

IN-PROMPT-YOU Moment 2

In what ways might you enhance the role of practice in your life?

(Write your answer below)

If you do not do your homework you are not going to do your best on the test. If you do not go to your scheduled basketball practice you will not be the best point guard you can be. If you don't seek opportunities to speak in front of crowds you won't become a powerful motivational speaker. If you are asleep while you should be writing, your world renowned poem you may never get the opportunity again.

Many talented people have not reached their true potential because they do not consistently practice. Today you have to decide if you will be like the boxer described above that practices every day consistently. Can I be honest with you? There is never a convenient time for you to practice. You have to create time by eliminating the things in your life that distract you from being a better version of yourself.

If entertainment prohibits you from practicing, remove it from your day. If unproductive affiliations distract you from developing your craft break away from the group. In the future, you will have plenty of time for entertainment while you are succeeding because of your commitment to practice routinely. Remember this phrase as you begin to implement practice in your daily life,

"Prior proper planning prevents poor performance."

Chapter 8

Polish

I remember going to the bowling alley often when I was a teenager with a group of other teens from my neighborhood. We would utilize public transportation to go to the bowling alley in the nearby suburbs. We would often put wagers on who would have the highest score at the end of the game. I remember that part vividly because I never won any of the games. One day an older gentleman notice how I was bowling and stopped to give me much needed pointers.

POLISH: make the surface of something smooth and shiny by rubbing it.

The first pointer he gave me was about my formation. He observed that my posture negatively impacted my performance. When I would go to bowl, I recklessly threw the bowling ball down the lane and prayed for the best. He took time to teach me how to stand properly and bowl accurately. The second piece of advice he gave me was to become one with the ball. You must have the same confused look on your face as I had when he shared this tip with me! The older gentleman was suggesting that in order for me to bowl properly not only did I need a great formation but I also needed to find a ball that I was comfortable with. I thought all bowling balls were the same prior to the much needed bowling wisdom he gave me.

From that time on I always examine the quality of each ball. I now carefully look for small cracks and dents every time I bowl. Lastly, he showed me how to use a bowling cloth to polish the ball. This process makes the ball flow smoothly down the lane. My bowling chronicles can serve as an example of how we should treat our voice. We owe it to ourselves and our audience to inspect the dents and scratches in our leadership that develop overtime. You must spend time examining it for dents and scratches that can manifest in the form of flaws and hindrances. An example of a hindrance is if you are an awesome speaker but you do not like to read. People will recognize you as a phenomenal orator but they will leave and tell others about the weakness of your points because it was not supported with quality thoughts and research.

Despite your success, you have the hindrance of being "ok" as a speaker. Nothing should agitate you more than being "ok". Now is the time to polish the potential and promise that is inside of you. During the polishing process it will be easy to give up when you first encounter friction. At that moment you must remember that friction may hurt but it is vital to your improvement. I challenge you to find a mentor that will help you become more polished. You will be amazed at who you will become and the impact you will have once you become polished.

Make-It-Happen Map 2

In the next 30 days , I will do the following to polish my skills and talents …	What resources are needed to accomplish this endeavor?
In the next 60 days , I will do the following to polish my skills and talents …	What resources are needed to accomplish this endeavor?
In the next 90 days , I will do the following to polish my skills and talents …	What resources are needed to accomplish this endeavor?

Chapter 9

Perpetuate

Wow, we have come to the final chapter in this 2nd

edition. By now you have been convinced that you are

a creative leader ready to change the world! You

should feel different about your life and your

leadership at this point. I know you are charged up

and ready to fly but before you do I want to give you the final **"p"**. This word takes the most work.

PERPETUATE: to cause something to last and indefinitely

The final **"p"** in this book is for perpetuate .This new change in your creative leadership cannot be just another phase that will fade over time. You must make it your business to diligently perpetuate every good gift and tremendous talent you have. I will be honest this step can be difficult and even seem impossible depending on how you look at it. Let's look at it through the lens of an amazing leader and catalyst for inclusive excellence, Dr. Felicia Brown-Haywood. She suggest that;

"If everyone that has breath would make a conscious decision to perpetuate love not hate, justice not injustice, humbleness not haughtiness, authenticity not deception and

community not chaos there will be no talk of ostracizing forty-seven percent of the population… We would all be perpetually included in the one hundred percent."

You will note that the quote above begins with two amazing words, "if everyone". From these initial words we see that the responsibility of perpetuation is on each and every one of us. If our world is to be a better place than we all must constantly lift our voice. The writer must write, the scientist must constantly search for life changing cures and you must do what you were called to do.

 The next words that jump out are "make a conscious decision". Here lies an important truth, we must have a mindset of success and determination. When you arise from your sleep you must tell yourself, **"I will be a great contributor to the world, I will transform the earth."** You must develop a heart that cannot be shaken. Your heart must be filled with the courage to be better today than you were yesterday. **Get Up!** Start to shift your attitude and actions today. You must make a conscious effort to not stay in the same place of comfort anymore.

Everything is an issue of the mind. Most people do not perpetuate their voice because they have not changed their mind about what they are doing. They may have changed their actions but not truly changed their beliefs. Most people quit the workout plan after eight days, diet after five days and the list goes on.

This book was written with you in mind. I wanted to give you practical tools that you can use to build your portfolio of achievement. In order to preserve the many insights you have gained, you must be consistent. Your future is calling, will you pick up? I cannot be there with you every time you want to give up on the project that you cannot seem to finish but I can leave you with a quick formula that I use in my own life.

Prior proper planning

Utilize your skills

Set your mind higher

Hold on to your dreams

Keep pushing and you will be the embodiment of the **"UNBOXED"** life.

About the Author

Dr. Marcellus C. Taylor is an innovative entrepreneur, teacher, author and strategist. He holds an earned doctorate in curriculum and instruction from Indiana University of Pennsylvania. He made history in his program when he graduated at the impressive age of 28. Dr. Taylor resides in Harrisburg, PA with his wife and their three sons.

Blossburg & Cedar LLC

Blossburg & Cedar is the result of when a challenge is met with a bold solution. Co-Founders Dr. Marcellus C. and Denise T. Taylor, MBA developed the concept of the firm while visiting close friends near Blossburg, PA. The primary mission of Blossburg & Cedar is to train organizations on how to effectively convert the vast amount of potential of their learners and employees into actualized success.

Grow with us:
grow@blossburgandcedar.com

www.ingramcontent.com/pod-product-compliance
Lightning Source LLC
Chambersburg PA
CBHW071109220526
45467CB00004B/1767